From Page to Network

FROM PAGE TO NETWORK

First edition. February 5, 2024.

Copyright © 2024 Maurice Philippe.

ISBN: 979-8224051779

Written by Maurice Philippe.

Table of Contents

Navigating the Digital Landscape of Storytelling

Maurice Philippe

❖ Introduction

A: Definition of "From Page to Network"

In the intricate dance between storytelling and technology, the phrase "From Page to Network" encapsulates a profound shift in the very essence of narrative creation and consumption. It serves as both a rallying cry and a compass, guiding us through the intricate web of changes that have unfolded in the world of storytelling.

"At its core, 'From Page to Network' signifies the transformative journey of storytelling from its traditional, linear roots on printed pages to the expansive, interconnected networks of the digital era. It is a narrative evolution that transcends the limitations of physical boundaries, weaving tales not just through words but through a dynamic interplay of multimedia elements, collaboration, and engagement in a vast, digital ecosystem."

This definition is a clarion call to reimagine storytelling as a dynamic, ever-evolving entity that adapts to the capabilities and possibilities offered by technology. No longer confined to the static nature of a single medium, stories now traverse a vast network, embracing a plethora of platforms and interactive features.

"From Page to Network" is an invitation to explore storytelling beyond the constraints of a book cover, to delve into narratives that sprawl across virtual realms, social media feeds, and immersive experiences. It signifies a departure from the one-way communication of traditional storytelling to a multidimensional conversation where creators and audiences coalesce in the digital tapestry of shared stories.

This chapter will unravel the layers of this definition, peeling back the intricacies to reveal how technology has become the loom on which the fabric of modern narratives is woven. As we navigate this evolving landscape, each subsequent chapter will shine a light on different facets of this transformation, offering a comprehensive understanding of the multifaceted journey "From Page to Network."

B: The Evolving Landscape of Storytelling

As we embark on the exploration of "From Page to Network," we find ourselves traversing a dynamic terrain shaped by the relentless march of time and technology.

The landscape of storytelling has undergone a profound metamorphosis, and in this chapter, we illuminate the contours of this evolution, tracing the journey from the simplicity of the written page to the intricate tapestry of the digital age.

The traditional landscape of storytelling, rooted in the tangible pages of books and the spoken word, has expanded into a vast and interconnected ecosystem.

The rise of digital platforms has ushered in an era where stories are not bound by the physical constraints of paper and ink. Instead, they unfold across a myriad of mediums, embracing the richness of multimedia elements, interactivity, and collaborative engagement.

In this digital era, storytelling is no longer a solitary experience confined to the hallowed space between the covers of a book. It has become a communal venture, where audiences participate actively in the creation, distribution, and interpretation of narratives.

The boundaries between creators and consumers have blurred, giving rise to a more democratic and inclusive form of storytelling.

The Evolving Landscape of Storytelling explores the shift from linear narratives to nonlinear, interactive experiences. The emergence of digital platforms has democratized the creation process, allowing storytellers to experiment with new forms and formats.

From Choose Your Own Adventure narratives to interactive multimedia experiences, the very structure of storytelling has undergone a revolution.

As we traverse this evolving landscape, we will encounter the power of storytelling to transcend its traditional constraints. We'll witness the fusion of technology and narrative craft, giving rise to new modes of expression and communication.

Join us as we navigate this shifting terrain, uncovering the threads that connect the past, present, and future of storytelling in the age of networks. The journey from the traditional page to the expansive digital landscape is a testament to the resilience and adaptability of storytelling, a phenomenon that continues to captivate and connect us in ways previously unimaginable.

C: The Impact of Technology on Narrative Forms

In the grand tapestry of storytelling, technology has emerged as a masterful weaver, reshaping the very fabric of narratives and fundamentally altering the way stories are conceived, consumed, and shared. This chapter delves into the profound impact of technology on the art of storytelling, examining the transformative influence that has propelled us from the simplicity of the written page to the interconnected networks of the digital age.

The Dynamic Interplay

Technology's impact is not merely a ripple on the surface but a seismic shift that has resonated through the core of storytelling. The digital age has ushered in an era where narratives are no longer static; they are dynamic, responsive, and participatory. The once passive audience has become an active participant, contributing to the narrative in unprecedented ways.

Redefining Consumption

The advent of technology has shattered the confines of traditional narrative consumption. No longer bound to physical books, audiences now engage with stories through a myriad of digital platforms, each offering a unique lens through which tales can be explored. E-books, audiobooks, and interactive experiences have become commonplace, providing a rich and varied landscape for audiences to navigate.

Breaking Down Barriers

Technology has not only transformed the way stories are told but has also dismantled barriers between creators and consumers. The democratization of content creation has given rise to a diverse array of voices, allowing stories from various perspectives to find their way to the forefront. This inclusivity has enriched the storytelling landscape, fostering a tapestry woven with threads of diverse cultures, experiences, and perspectives.

Interactivity and Immersion

The impact of technology is perhaps most palpable in the realms of interactivity and immersion. From virtual and augmented reality experiences that transport audiences to fantastical worlds, to interactive narratives that allow readers to shape the course of a story, technology has elevated storytelling to a multisensory and participatory experience.

Navigating Challenges

However, as we navigate this digital frontier, challenges arise. The rapid pace of technological evolution raises questions of accessibility, ethical considerations, and the preservation of traditional storytelling forms.

This chapter will explore the delicate balance between innovation and preservation, acknowledging both the opportunities and the responsibilities that come with the integration of technology into the art of storytelling.

Join us on this journey as we unravel the intricate relationship between technology and narrative forms. The impact of technology is not a static point in time but a continuous, dynamic force shaping the landscape of storytelling—an ever-evolving narrative that invites us to explore, adapt, and redefine the very essence of our shared stories.

Chapter (1) The Traditional Page

A: Historical Overview of Storytelling through Written Pages

In the vast expanse of human history, the art of storytelling has found its enduring expression through the written word. As we embark on a historical overview, we venture into the epochs where stories were inscribed on pages, weaving a narrative tapestry that transcends time and cultures.

- **The Birth of the Written Word**

Our journey commences with the birth of written language—an epochal moment in the human saga. From the cuneiform tablets of Mesopotamia to the hieroglyphics adorning the walls of ancient Egyptian tombs, early civilizations etched their stories into the annals of time. The development of scripts and writing systems became a conduit for the transmission of myths, legends, and the collective wisdom of societies.

- **Manuscripts and the Illuminated Age**

The medieval period ushered in a new chapter, marked by the meticulous creation of manuscripts. Monastic scribes, often cloistered in scriptoriums, crafted ornate pages adorned with intricate illustrations. The illuminated manuscripts, with their vibrant colors and elaborate decorations, transformed storytelling into a visual spectacle. Each page became a work of art, preserving tales that were passed down through generations.

- **The Printing Revolution**

The turning point in the evolution of storytelling arrived with the invention of the printing press by Johannes Gutenberg in the 15th century. This technological marvel democratized access to written knowledge, making books more widely available. The mass production of printed material fueled the Renaissance, sparking an intellectual and cultural renaissance as stories, ideas, and knowledge spread rapidly across continents.

- **Literary Classics and the Rise of the Novel**

As societies progressed, so did the complexity of narratives. The 18th and 19th centuries witnessed the rise of literary classics—timeless works that explored the depths of human experience. From the epics of Homer to the plays of Shakespeare, storytelling matured as a sophisticated art form. The novel, a novel medium in itself, emerged as a dominant force, providing a platform for authors to weave intricate plots and explore the intricacies of character and society.

- **Cultural Narratives and Global Influence**

Through the colonial era and into the modern age, written pages became not just repositories of stories but powerful tools for shaping cultural narratives. Writers from diverse backgrounds brought forth their unique perspectives, influencing global discourse and fostering cross-cultural understanding. The printed page became a bridge connecting different corners of the world through shared stories.

This historical overview serves as a foundation, revealing the profound role that written pages have played in human civilization.

From the earliest symbols etched on stone tablets to the globally influential novels of today, the evolution of storytelling through written pages stands as a testament to the enduring power of the written word—a power that continues to captivate hearts and minds across the ages. Join us as we turn the pages of history to uncover the roots of this timeless art.

B: The Power of Printed Words and the Magic of Books

In the hallowed halls of literature, the power of printed words and the enchantment of books have cast a spell over generations, creating a timeless allure that transcends the mere arrangement of ink on paper. This chapter delves into the profound impact of the printing press, the allure of physical books, and the magical realms they open to readers.

- **The Printing Press: A Revolution Unleashed**

Johannes Gutenberg's invention of the printing press in the 15th century marked a watershed moment in human history. Suddenly, the production of books became a scalable endeavor, and the dissemination of knowledge reached unprecedented heights. The printed word ceased to be a luxury accessible only to the elite, evolving into a democratic force that empowered the masses.

- **Democratizing Knowledge and Igniting Revolutions**

The power of printed words lay not only in their accessibility but also in their ability to ignite revolutions. Pamphlets, manifestos, and treatises printed during times of political upheaval became weapons of change. The Enlightenment era saw an explosion of printed material challenging the status quo, fostering critical thinking, and laying the groundwork for social and intellectual revolutions.

- **The Tangibility of Books: A Sensorial Experience**

While the digital age has ushered in new forms of reading, the allure of physical books endures. This section explores the sensorial experience of holding a book—the weight of its pages, the texture of its cover, the aroma of ink and paper. The act of turning each page becomes a tactile journey, and the tangible nature of books enhances the immersive quality of storytelling.

- **The Book as a Portal to Other Worlds**

Books possess a transformative magic, acting as portals to realms beyond our own. This subsection explores how literature, through its printed medium, enables readers to escape into fantastical worlds, traverse through time, or delve into the depths of the human psyche. The immersive power of storytelling unfolds within the pages, creating an intimate connection between the author's imagination and the reader's.

- **The Artistry of Books: Illuminated Manuscripts to Cover Design**

Beyond the written word, the artistry of books plays a pivotal role in their enchantment. From the illuminated manuscripts of medieval times to contemporary cover designs, books are visual expressions of creativity. The marriage of art and literature enhances the storytelling experience, making each book not only a vessel of words but a work of art in its own right.

In exploring the power of printed words and the magic of books, this chapter invites readers to reflect on the profound influence of the physical medium. As we turn the pages of history, we uncover not just stories but the transformative force that literature exerts on individuals and societies. Join us in a celebration of the enduring enchantment that resides within the pages of books—a magic that continues to captivate hearts and minds across cultures and generations.

C: Classic Storytelling Techniques and Their Endurance

Within the realm of the traditional page, storytelling emerges as an art form woven with timeless techniques that have weathered the sands of changing eras. This chapter illuminates the enduring nature of classic storytelling techniques, exploring how they have not only stood the test of time but continue to shape narratives in the modern age.

- **The Hero's Journey: A Mythic Blueprint**

At the heart of classic storytelling lies the hero's journey, an archetypal narrative structure that transcends cultural boundaries. From ancient myths to contemporary tales, this section delves into the stages of the hero's journey—call to adventure, trials, and ultimate transformation. We explore how protagonists, whether ancient heroes or modern characters, embark on quests that mirror the human experience and resonate with readers across generations.

- **The Three-Act Structure: Foundations of Drama**

The three-act structure, a cornerstone of storytelling, unfolds like a well-choreographed dance—establishing equilibrium, introducing conflict, and resolving tension. We delve into the origins of this narrative structure, tracing its roots from Aristotle's dramatic principles to its ubiquitous presence in plays, novels, and films. The enduring appeal of the three-act structure lies in its ability to create a compelling rhythm that captivates audiences and sustains engagement.

- **Archetypes and Symbols: Universality in Storytelling**

Beyond the plot, classic storytelling relies on the use of archetypes and symbols—universal elements that tap into the collective unconscious. This segment explores the enduring power of archetypal characters such as the hero, the mentor, and the villain. Additionally, it delves into symbols that resonate across cultures, adding layers of meaning to narratives. These elements serve as a shared language, fostering connections between stories and the human psyche.

- **Narrative Techniques: Show, Don't Tell**

Crafting vivid and immersive worlds requires mastery of narrative techniques. The principle of "show, don't tell" takes center stage as we explore how authors paint rich landscapes and evoke emotions through descriptive prose and nuanced dialogue. This section examines how the careful use of language, pacing, and perspective creates a symphony of words that transcends the page, resonating in the minds of readers.

- **Timeless Themes: Love, Loss, and Redemption**

Themes such as love, loss, and redemption echo through the corridors of classic literature. This part of the chapter delves into the enduring appeal of these timeless themes, examining how they serve as touchstones for human experience. Whether in ancient epics or contemporary novels, stories that explore the complexities of human relationships and the journey towards redemption continue to strike a chord with audiences.

As we navigate the traditional page, these classic storytelling techniques emerge not as relics of a bygone era but as guiding stars that illuminate the path for storytellers across time. Join us in a celebration of the enduring resonance of these techniques, as they continue to shape narratives, capturing the imaginations of readers and ensuring that the magic of storytelling remains evergreen.

Chapter (2) The Rise of Digital Storytelling

A: Emergence of Digital Platforms and Their Influence

In the ever-expanding universe of storytelling, the emergence of digital platforms has been a catalyst for a transformative narrative revolution. This section of the chapter unveils the early days of online storytelling, exploring the birth of digital platforms and their profound influence on the way stories are conceived, shared, and consumed.

- **The Dawn of Digital Storytelling**

As the internet gained prominence, it became a fertile ground for a burgeoning community of storytellers. Early websites, blogs, and forums became the digital pages where narratives unfolded. This subsection traces the initial forays into online storytelling, from experimental narratives to the first serialized web novels. The freedom afforded by digital platforms allowed storytellers to experiment with new forms, paving the way for a diverse and dynamic narrative landscape.

- **The Democratization of Storytelling**

Digital platforms democratized storytelling, breaking down barriers to entry and providing a global stage for voices that might have remained unheard in traditional publishing circles. The rise of platforms like Wattpad and Medium empowered both aspiring and established writers, enabling them to reach audiences far beyond geographical boundaries. This section delves into how these platforms became catalysts for a storytelling renaissance, fostering creativity and diversity.

- **Collaborative Storytelling and Community Building**

Digital platforms not only facilitated individual storytelling but also gave rise to collaborative efforts and community building. Online communities formed around shared interests, genres, and themes, providing a space for writers and readers to connect, discuss, and co-create. The interactive nature of these platforms blurred the lines between creator and audience, transforming storytelling into a communal experience.

- **Multimedia Storytelling: Beyond Words**

With the integration of multimedia elements, digital platforms expanded the storytelling palette. This subsection explores how images, videos, and interactive features became integral to narratives. From multimedia-enhanced webcomics to immersive storytelling experiences that incorporate sound and visuals, storytellers found new ways to engage and captivate their audiences.

- **Challenges and Opportunities in the Digital Landscape**

The digital era brought with it a unique set of challenges and opportunities. This section examines issues such as information overload, the need for digital literacy, and the evolving nature of copyright in the online space. Simultaneously, it highlights the opportunities for innovative storytelling, audience engagement, and the exploration of niche genres that thrive in the vastness of the digital landscape.

As we navigate the emergence of digital platforms, this chapter unfolds the narrative of a profound shift in storytelling paradigms. Join us in exploring the digital frontier, where the democratization of storytelling and the fusion of multimedia elements have ushered in a new era of narrative possibilities. The journey from traditional pages to the vast expanses of the digital landscape is a testament to the evolving nature of storytelling in the interconnected age.

B: Interactivity in Storytelling: Choose Your Own Adventure Narratives

In the realm of digital storytelling, a revolutionary shift occurred with the advent of interactivity, transforming narratives from static experiences into dynamic, participatory journeys. This section of the chapter immerses us in the evolution of interactive storytelling, with a particular focus on the captivating world of Choose Your Own Adventure narratives.

- **Origins of Interactive Storytelling**

The concept of interactive storytelling traces its roots back to the traditional "Choose Your Own Adventure" (CYOA) books. This subsection delves into the origins of this format, exploring how it emerged as a pioneering experiment in reader agency. From its early incarnations in print to its subsequent migration to digital platforms, the CYOA narrative structure became a playground for exploring the endless possibilities of reader choices.

- **From Print to Pixels: Digital Resurgence**

The transition to digital platforms marked a renaissance for interactive storytelling. This part of the chapter unfolds the journey of CYOA narratives as they migrated from the pages of books to the screens of computers and mobile devices. The integration of hyperlinks, decision trees, and multimedia elements in digital formats allowed for a more seamless and immersive interactive experience.

- **Agency and Empowerment: Readers as Co-Creators**

Interactive storytelling shifted the balance of power between storyteller and audience. Readers were no longer passive observers but active participants, influencing the direction of the narrative with their choices. This section explores how interactivity empowers readers, turning them into co-creators who shape the story's unfolding, fostering a sense of agency and immersion.

- **Beyond Binary Choices: Nuanced Decision-Making**

The evolution of interactivity goes beyond simple binary choices. This subsection delves into the sophistication of decision-making within interactive narratives, where choices are not just about diverging paths but also influence character development, plot intricacies, and even the emotional tone of the story. The narrative branches become intricate webs, reflecting the complexity of the human experience.

- **The Digital Renaissance: Platforms and Possibilities**

Digital platforms opened up new horizons for interactive storytelling. This section explores the diverse platforms that embraced this format, from web-based interactive fiction to mobile apps and immersive experiences in virtual reality. The digital renaissance of interactive storytelling expanded its reach, captivating audiences across different demographics and genres.

- **Challenges and Innovations: Navigating the Interactive Landscape**

While interactivity brought a wave of innovation, it also posed unique challenges. This part of the chapter examines issues such as narrative coherence, the balance between freedom and structure, and the technical complexities of designing interactive experiences. Yet, it celebrates the creative solutions and innovations that storytellers have employed to navigate these challenges.

As we navigate the realm of interactivity in storytelling, this chapter invites readers to choose their own adventure within the evolving landscape of narratives. Join us on a journey where every click, tap, or decision leads to a new twist in the tale, as we explore the boundless possibilities and immersive experiences offered by interactive storytelling in the digital age.

C: The Evolution of E-books and Audiobooks

In the digital age, the traditional page underwent a transformative metamorphosis, giving rise to new mediums that transcended the physical constraints of printed books. This section of the chapter unfolds the captivating narrative of the evolution of e-books and audiobooks, exploring how these digital formats have reshaped the landscape of storytelling.

- **The Advent of E-books: Portability and Accessibility**

The digital revolution brought forth a revolutionary transformation in how we read with the advent of e-books. This subsection delves into the early days of e-books, exploring how digitization made literature portable and accessible to a global audience. The ease of carrying an entire library in a pocket-sized device marked a paradigm shift, allowing readers to explore a vast array of titles with unprecedented convenience.

- **Digital Reading Experience: Beyond the Traditional Page**

The evolution of e-books extended beyond the mere replication of printed pages on a screen. This part of the chapter illuminates how digital reading experiences enhanced storytelling through features like adjustable fonts, interactive elements, and multimedia enhancements. E-books became a canvas for innovation, offering readers a dynamic and customizable engagement with narratives.

- **Audiobooks: The Resurgence of Oral Storytelling**

While e-books catered to the visual senses, audiobooks emerged as a powerful medium that appealed to the auditory senses. This subsection explores the resurgence of oral storytelling through audiobooks, tracing their roots from cassette tapes to the digital platforms of today. The immersive experience of having stories narrated by skilled performers breathed new life into classic and contemporary tales.

- **Narration as Art: The Rise of Audiobook Performers**

Audiobooks introduced a new dimension to storytelling—the art of narration. This section explores how skilled performers and actors became an integral part of audiobook production, bringing characters to life with nuanced performances. The narration itself became an art form, enhancing the emotional resonance of the narrative and creating a more intimate connection between the storyteller and the audience.

- **Digital Publishing and Industry Transformation**

The rise of e-books and audiobooks revolutionized the traditional publishing industry. This subsection examines how digital formats provided new avenues for both established authors and emerging voices. Self-publishing platforms and digital distribution channels democratized access to the literary world, fostering a diverse and dynamic landscape of storytellers.

- **The Multimodal Future: Convergence of Text and Audio**

As technology advanced, the lines between e-books and audiobooks blurred, giving rise to a multimodal future. This part of the chapter explores how platforms seamlessly integrated text and audio, offering readers the flexibility to switch between reading and listening. The convergence of these formats created a holistic and inclusive reading experience.

The evolution of e-books and audiobooks is a testament to the dynamic interplay between technology and storytelling. Join us in unraveling the narrative threads that weave through these digital formats, as we explore the ways in which they have transformed the reading experience and expanded the horizons of narrative expression in the digital age.

Chapter (3) Social Media Narratives

A: Micro-stories on Social Platforms

In the fast-paced realms of social media, storytelling has undergone a remarkable transformation, giving rise to the art of micro-stories. This section of the chapter immerses us in the world of concise narratives that unfold in the dynamic landscape of social platforms. From Twitter's succinct tales to Instagram's visual narratives, we explore the allure and impact of micro-stories in the digital age.

- **Twitterature: Crafting in 280 Characters**

At the forefront of micro-storytelling, Twitter stands as a unique canvas where brevity becomes an art form. In the realm of Twitterature, storytellers weave tales within the constraints of 280 characters. This subsection explores how writers embrace the challenge of distilling narratives into concise gems, each tweet a snapshot of a larger story. The immediacy and shareability of micro-stories on Twitter have transformed the platform into a dynamic literary landscape, where stories unfold in the blink of an eye.

- **Instagram's Visual Stories: Beyond the Grid**

Instagram, a visual playground, has redefined storytelling through imagery and multimedia. We delve into the world of visual narratives, where each image, video, or carousel becomes a chapter in a larger story. From immersive grid layouts to the ephemeral storytelling of Instagram Stories, we explore how visual elements become powerful tools for crafting narratives that resonate with a global audience.

- **Snapchat's Disappearing Act: Evolving Narratives**

Snapchat introduced a new dimension to micro-storytelling with its disappearing content. This subsection unravels the dynamics of ephemeral narratives, where stories vanish after a brief moment. The temporality of Snapchat stories adds an element of urgency and authenticity, creating a unique space for unfiltered and candid micro-stories that captivate audiences in real-time.

- **Challenges and Innovations in Micro-storytelling**

While micro-stories offer a captivating form of storytelling, they come with their own set of challenges. This part of the chapter examines the complexities of conveying depth and emotion within limited characters or visual elements. It also celebrates the creative solutions and innovations that storytellers employ to make a profound impact within the constraints of micro-storytelling.

As we navigate the landscape of micro-stories on social platforms, this chapter invites readers to appreciate the artistry of brevity and the dynamic narratives that unfold in the digital agora. Join us in exploring the ways in which storytellers master the craft of concise storytelling, leaving a lasting impression in the ephemeral spaces of social media.

B: Influencer Culture and Its Impact on Storytelling

In the interconnected world of social media, a new breed of storytellers has emerged—social media influencers. This section of the chapter delves into the phenomenon of influencer culture, exploring how these digital architects of narratives have reshaped storytelling, leaving an indelible mark on trends, culture, and the way stories are told in the digital age.

- **From Followers to Storytellers: The Rise of Influencers**

Social media influencers have transcended the role of mere trendsetters to become modern-day storytellers. This subsection unravels the evolution of influencers, examining how they craft compelling narratives around their lifestyles, interests, and experiences. The authenticity and relatability of influencers create a unique bond with their followers, transforming them from passive spectators into active participants in the unfolding narrative.

- **The Personal as Narrative: Lifestyle Storytelling**

Influencers often blur the lines between personal and public life, turning their everyday experiences into captivating stories. We explore how lifestyle storytelling has become a cornerstone of influencer culture, with influencers sharing not just products but narratives that resonate with authenticity. The personalization of stories creates a sense of intimacy, making followers feel like they are part of the influencer's journey.

- **Influencers as Brand Storytellers**

The narrative power of influencers extends beyond personal stories to brand collaborations. This part of the chapter delves into how influencers seamlessly integrate brand stories into their personal narratives, creating a symbiotic relationship that benefits both storyteller and brand. The art of influencer marketing has become instrumental in shaping consumer narratives in the digital age, with influencers serving as conduits for brand messages.

- **The Influence of Visual Storytelling**

Influencer culture is intrinsically tied to visual storytelling. This subsection explores how influencers leverage visuals—photographs, videos, and multimedia content—to enhance their narratives. The carefully curated aesthetics of an influencer's feed or channel contribute to the overall storytelling experience, creating a cohesive and visually compelling narrative.

- **Challenges and Critiques of Influencer Culture**

While influencer culture has become a dominant force, it is not without its challenges and critiques. This section examines issues such as authenticity, the blurred lines between advertising and storytelling, and the potential impact of influencer narratives on societal norms. The chapter navigates the nuanced landscape of influencer culture, acknowledging both its positive contributions and areas that warrant critical examination.

As we navigate the realm of influencer culture, this chapter invites readers to explore the transformative impact of these modern storytellers. Join us in uncovering the ways in which influencers have redefined the art of storytelling, shaping not only individual narratives but also influencing cultural trends and societal perspectives in the interconnected digital landscape.

C: The Role of User-Generated Content in Shaping Narratives

In the participatory landscape of social media, user-generated content (UGC) has become a driving force, reshaping narratives, and democratizing the storytelling experience. This section of the chapter immerses us in the transformative role of UGC, exploring how users contribute to and shape the stories told on social platforms.

- **Crowdsourced Narratives: Shaping Collective Stories**

Social media platforms provide fertile ground for crowdsourced narratives, where users collectively contribute to the creation of stories. From collaborative writing projects to community-driven storytelling, this subsection delves into how UGC transforms storytelling from a solitary pursuit into a communal experience. Users become not only consumers but active contributors, shaping the narrative landscape through their diverse voices.

- **Virality and Memes: The Swift Evolution of Narratives**

Memes and viral content act as catalysts in the swift evolution of narratives. This part of the chapter examines how user-generated content, in the form of memes and viral challenges, can rapidly shape and redefine cultural narratives. The participatory nature of these trends turns users into co-creators of cultural moments, influencing not only online discourse but also societal conversations.

- **User-Generated Aesthetics: The Visual Language of Narratives**

Beyond written content, users contribute to storytelling through the creation of visual aesthetics. This subsection explores how platforms like Pinterest and Tumblr become canvases for users to curate and share visual narratives. The act of image curation, from mood boards to thematic collections, allows users to express themselves and contribute to the visual language of storytelling.

- **Authenticity and Connection: The Power of User Stories**

User-generated content often thrives on authenticity and connection. We delve into how users sharing personal stories—whether through blog posts, vlogs, or personal essays—create a rich tapestry of diverse experiences. The authenticity of these narratives fosters a sense of connection among users, breaking down barriers and forging a community built on shared stories.

- **Challenges and Ethics of User-Generated Content**

While UGC opens new avenues for storytelling, it also brings forth challenges and ethical considerations. This section examines issues such as content moderation, misinformation, and the potential for harmful narratives. Navigating the ethical dimensions of UGC is crucial in ensuring that user-generated content contributes positively to the narrative landscape.

As we navigate the dynamic interplay of user-generated content in shaping narratives, this chapter invites readers to appreciate the democratization of storytelling. Join us in exploring the ways in which users actively contribute to the collective narrative, shaping digital discourse, and fostering a sense of community through their diverse stories.

Chapter (4) Transmedia Storytelling

A: Definition and Examples of Transmedia Storytelling

Defining Transmedia Storytelling

Transmedia storytelling is a narrative strategy that involves the seamless integration and expansion of a story across multiple media platforms and formats. Instead of confining the narrative to a single medium, transmedia storytelling leverages the strengths of each platform to create a more immersive and interconnected experience. This approach invites audiences to explore the storyworld through various entry points, fostering engagement and participation.

Examples of Transmedia Narratives

1. **"Star Wars" Universe:**

- Films: The core narrative unfolds in the iconic film series.
- Books: Novels delve into character backstories, extending the lore.
- TV Shows: Series like "The Mandalorian" introduce new characters and plotlines.
- Comics: Comic series explore additional adventures and perspectives.
- Video Games: Games allow players to experience the Star Wars universe firsthand.

1. **"The Matrix" Franchise:**

- Films: The main storyline is presented through the film trilogy.
- Animatrix: An animated anthology expands on the world's history and characters.

- Video Games: Games provide interactive experiences within the Matrix.
- Comics: Graphic novels offer supplementary stories and insights.

1. **"The Blair Witch Project":**

- Film: The original film introduces the mysterious Blair Witch.
- Web Content: Online forums and websites expand the urban legend.
- Video Games: Games like "Blair Witch" offer interactive horror experiences.
- VR Experiences: Virtual reality immerses users in the eerie Blair Witch forest.

These examples illustrate how transmedia storytelling allows narratives to transcend traditional boundaries, offering audiences a more comprehensive and engaging experience by combining various media forms.

As we navigate the concept and examples of transmedia storytelling, this chapter invites readers to explore the interconnected narrative landscape that unfolds across films, books, games, and other media platforms. Join us in unraveling the intricate threads of storytelling that extend beyond the confines of a single medium, creating a cohesive and immersive tapestry for audiences to explore.

B: Expanding Narratives Across Various Media Channels

Transmedia storytelling unfolds like a rich tapestry, weaving its narrative threads across diverse media channels. This section explores how transmedia narratives extend beyond traditional mediums, creating a dynamic and interconnected storytelling experience.

Films and TV Shows: The Core Narrative

In many transmedia narratives, films and TV shows serve as the cornerstone, introducing audiences to the central storyline, characters, and themes. These visual mediums establish the foundation upon which the transmedia storyworld is built, providing a shared starting point for audiences.

Books and Novels: Deepening the Lore

Transmedia storytelling often extends into literature, using books and novels to delve deeper into the lore of the story. Written works offer opportunities to explore character backgrounds, intricate plot details, and additional layers of narrative complexity, enriching the overall storytelling experience.

Video Games and Interactive Experiences: Player Agency

Interactive media, particularly video games, becomes a vital channel for transmedia storytelling. These experiences empower audiences with agency, allowing them to influence the narrative through their choices and actions. Video games become immersive platforms where players actively shape the story, contributing to a more engaging and personalized experience.

Social Media and Web Content: Real-time Interaction

Transmedia narratives leverage social media and web content to maintain real-time interaction with audiences. Platforms like Twitter, Instagram, and dedicated websites become spaces for delivering supplementary content, updates, and interactive elements. Audiences can engage with the storyworld beyond traditional release schedules, fostering a sense of ongoing participation.

Alternate Reality Games (ARGs): Immersive Exploration

The incorporation of alternate reality games (ARGs) adds an interactive layer to transmedia storytelling. These games extend the narrative into the real world, inviting audiences to solve puzzles, follow clues, and actively participate in the unfolding story. ARGs blur the lines between fiction and reality, providing a unique and immersive storytelling experience.

Virtual and Augmented Reality: Immersive Storyworlds

The integration of virtual and augmented reality technologies introduces a new dimension to transmedia storytelling. These immersive technologies enable audiences to step directly into the storyworld, offering a heightened level of engagement and presence. Virtual and augmented reality experiences create a more visceral and interactive connection with the narrative.

As we explore the expansion of narratives across various media channels in transmedia storytelling, this chapter invites readers to appreciate the versatility and richness of storytelling experiences that unfold beyond the boundaries of individual mediums. Join us in unraveling the interconnected narrative threads that span films, books, games, social media, and immersive technologies, creating a holistic and engaging storyworld for audiences to explore.

C: Engaging Audiences Through a Multi-platform Approach

Transmedia storytelling is distinguished by its ability to captivate audiences through a multi-platform approach. This section delves into the strategies and techniques employed to engage audiences across diverse channels, creating an immersive and participatory narrative experience.

- **Social Media and Web Content: Real-time Interaction**

Interactive Updates and Teasers

Social media platforms serve as dynamic spaces for real-time interaction. Transmedia narratives leverage platforms like Twitter, Instagram, and Facebook to provide interactive updates, teasers, and behind-the-scenes content. This approach keeps audiences engaged between major releases, fostering anticipation and maintaining a continuous connection.

Dedicated Websites and Forums

In addition to social media, dedicated websites and forums become hubs for extended storytelling. These platforms offer a centralized space for fans to explore supplementary content, discuss theories, and participate in community-driven activities. The creation of online communities enhances the sense of belonging and shared enthusiasm among audiences.

- **Alternate Reality Games (ARGs): Immersive Exploration**

Puzzle-solving and Clue-following

Transmedia storytelling utilizes ARGs to immerse audiences in an interactive and immersive exploration of the narrative. ARGs often involve puzzle-solving and clue-following, encouraging participants to collaborate and unravel mysteries. The real-world engagement adds layers of complexity to the narrative, turning audiences into active participants in the storytelling process.

Real-world Events and Challenges

ARGs extend into the real world, incorporating events and challenges that blur the boundaries between fiction and reality. Participants may find themselves attending live events, receiving mysterious packages, or encountering challenges in their day-to-day lives. This blend of the virtual and real realms enhances the immersive nature of the transmedia experience.

- **Virtual and Augmented Reality: Immersive Storyworlds**

Interactive VR and AR Experiences

Virtual and augmented reality technologies offer a heightened level of immersion, allowing audiences to step directly into the storyworld. Interactive VR and AR experiences enable users to explore environments, interact with characters, and contribute to the unfolding narrative. This hands-on engagement creates a sense of presence and agency, fostering a deeper connection with the story.

Branded Apps and Experiences

Transmedia storytelling extends into the realm of mobile apps and immersive experiences. Branded apps provide audiences with additional content, interactive elements, and exclusive insights into the story. These apps serve as portals to the transmedia narrative, offering users a personalized and customizable journey through the storyworld.

As we navigate the multi-platform approach of transmedia storytelling, this chapter invites readers to explore the diverse channels through which narratives unfold. Join us in unraveling the strategies that captivate audiences, fostering a sense of active participation and immersion in the interconnected and expansive storyworlds crafted through social media, alternate reality games, and immersive technologies.

Chapter (5) Virtual and Augmented Reality

A: Immersive Storytelling Experiences

Virtual and augmented reality technologies have ushered in a new era of storytelling, providing audiences with immersive experiences that go beyond the traditional boundaries of narrative. This section of the chapter delves into the captivating world of immersive storytelling in virtual and augmented reality.

VR: Stepping into the Storyworld

1. Spatial Presence and Immersion:

Virtual reality enables audiences to step into a meticulously crafted storyworld, experiencing a profound sense of spatial presence. Users find themselves surrounded by the narrative environment, whether it's a fantastical realm, historical setting, or futuristic landscape. The immersion extends beyond visual elements, incorporating spatial audio to enhance the sensory experience.

2. Interactivity and Agency:

VR introduces a level of interactivity that transforms audiences from passive observers to active participants. Users can interact with objects, characters, and the environment, influencing the direction of the narrative. This hands-on agency creates a dynamic storytelling experience, allowing individuals to shape the story based on their choices and actions.

3. Emotional Engagement:

The immersive nature of VR fosters emotional engagement by creating a direct connection between the audience and the narrative. Whether it's empathizing with characters or experiencing the intensity of a storyline, VR evokes emotions in a way that traditional media cannot.

The combination of spatial storytelling and emotional engagement makes VR a powerful medium for narrative experiences.

AR: Overlapping Fiction with Reality

1. Blending Fiction and Reality:

Augmented reality overlays fictional elements onto the real world, creating a seamless blend of fiction and reality. AR storytelling takes place within the user's immediate surroundings, with digital elements seamlessly integrated into the physical environment. This blending of worlds enhances the sense of magic and wonder in storytelling.

2. Location-based Narratives:

AR opens up possibilities for location-based storytelling, where narratives unfold based on the user's physical location. Whether it's discovering hidden clues in a city or interacting with virtual characters at specific landmarks, location-based AR narratives transform ordinary spaces into stages for immersive storytelling.

3. Interactive Elements in Everyday Environments:

AR experiences encourage audiences to interact with digital elements overlaid on everyday objects and environments. Users may find themselves solving puzzles, uncovering hidden stories, or interacting with characters seamlessly integrated into their surroundings. This interactive layer adds depth to the narrative experience.

As we immerse ourselves in the possibilities of virtual and augmented reality storytelling, this chapter invites readers to envision the transformative power of these technologies in creating narrative worlds that blur the lines between the virtual and the real. Join us in exploring the rich tapestry of immersive storytelling, where the boundaries of fiction and reality dissolve, and narratives come to life in unprecedented ways.

B: The Potential of VR and AR in Narrative Creation

Virtual and augmented reality (VR and AR) technologies offer unprecedented potential in reshaping the landscape of narrative creation. This section explores the innovative ways in which VR and AR contribute to the storytelling process, from interactive narratives to spatial storytelling.

Interactive Storytelling in VR

1. User Agency and Decision-making:

VR introduces a level of interactivity that allows users to actively shape the narrative. Through decision-making and interactive elements, users become protagonists in the story, influencing the direction and outcomes. This potential for user agency enhances engagement and offers a personalized storytelling experience.

2. Adaptive Narratives:

The dynamic nature of VR enables the creation of adaptive narratives. Stories can evolve based on user choices, creating branching paths and multiple story outcomes. Adaptive narratives respond to user actions, fostering a sense of immersion and personalization as the story unfolds in response to individual decisions.

3. Spatial Storytelling:

VR goes beyond traditional linear narratives by incorporating spatial storytelling. Users can explore and interact with the narrative environment in three-dimensional space. This spatial storytelling allows for a more holistic and immersive experience, where the physicality of the space becomes an integral part of the narrative.

Spatial Storytelling with AR

1. Overlaying Fiction onto Reality:

AR technologies overlay fictional elements onto the real world, creating a narrative that coexists with the user's immediate environment. This potential allows storytellers to leverage real-world locations, objects, and landmarks as integral components of the narrative, blurring the boundaries between fiction and reality.

2. Location-based Narratives:

AR introduces the concept of location-based narratives, where the story unfolds based on the user's physical location. This creates a dynamic storytelling experience tied to specific places, encouraging users to explore and engage with the narrative in context. Location-based AR narratives transform everyday spaces into storytelling canvases.

3. Interactive Elements in Everyday Environments:

AR narratives encourage users to interact with digital elements seamlessly integrated into everyday environments. Whether it's solving puzzles, discovering hidden messages, or interacting with virtual characters, these interactive elements bring the narrative to life in the user's immediate surroundings.

Case Studies of Successful Virtual Storytelling Projects

1. "The Blue Planet VR Experience"

Immersive Exploration: This VR project takes users on a deep-sea journey, allowing them to explore marine life in a fully immersive environment.

Educational Impact: By combining VR with educational content, the experience not only entertains but also educates users about marine ecosystems and conservation.

2. "Pokemon GO"

AR and Location-based Storytelling: "Pokemon GO" blends AR with location-based storytelling, transforming the real world into a virtual playground for users to discover and catch Pokemon.

Community Engagement: The game fosters a global community of players, encouraging social interaction and collaboration in the pursuit of shared narrative goals.

3. "Wolves in the Walls"

VR and Interactive Narratives: This VR experience is an interactive adaptation of Neil Gaiman's book, allowing users to engage with the story's protagonist, Lucy, and influence the narrative direction.

Blurring Realities: By blurring the line between the virtual and real worlds, "Wolves in the Walls" exemplifies how VR can create emotionally resonant and participatory narratives.

As we explore the potential of VR and AR in narrative creation, this chapter invites readers to envision a future where storytelling becomes a fully immersive and interactive experience. Join us in unraveling the ways in which these technologies shape the creation of narratives, offering new possibilities for engagement, agency, and storytelling innovation.

C: Case Studies of Successful Virtual Storytelling Projects

The world of virtual storytelling has witnessed remarkable projects that showcase the potential and impact of immersive experiences. This section explores case studies of successful virtual storytelling projects, highlighting their innovative approaches and the unique narrative possibilities offered by virtual reality (VR) and augmented reality (AR).

1. "The Blue Planet VR Experience"

Overview:

Immersive Exploration: This VR project takes users on a deep-sea journey, allowing them to explore marine life in a fully immersive environment.

Educational Impact: By combining VR with educational content, the experience not only entertains but also educates users about marine ecosystems and conservation.

Success Factors:

Educational Integration: The project seamlessly integrates entertainment with educational objectives, making it a valuable tool for learning about marine biology and environmental conservation.

Immersive Engagement: The immersive nature of the VR experience enhances engagement by providing users with a firsthand encounter with marine life, fostering a deeper connection to the subject matter.

2. "Pokemon GO"

Overview:

AR and Location-based Storytelling: "Pokemon GO" revolutionized mobile gaming by blending AR with location-based storytelling. Players explore real-world locations to discover and catch virtual Pokemon.

Community Engagement: The game fosters a global community of players, encouraging social interaction and collaboration in the pursuit of shared narrative goals.

Success Factors:

Real-world Integration: "Pokemon GO" successfully integrates the virtual and real worlds, encouraging players to explore their surroundings and fostering a sense of adventure.

Community Building: The game's design encourages social interaction and collaboration, turning the narrative into a collective experience shared by a global community of players.

3. "Wolves in the Walls"

Overview:

VR and Interactive Narratives: This VR experience is an interactive adaptation of Neil Gaiman's book, allowing users to engage with the story's protagonist, Lucy, and influence the narrative direction.

Blurring Realities: By blurring the line between the virtual and real worlds, "Wolves in the Walls" exemplifies how VR can create emotionally resonant and participatory narratives.

Success Factors:

User Agency: The interactive nature of the VR experience provides users with agency, allowing them to influence the story and engage with the narrative on a personal level.

Emotional Resonance: "Wolves in the Walls" leverages the immersive capabilities of VR to create emotionally resonant storytelling, enhancing the user's connection to the characters and plot.

These case studies exemplify the diverse ways in which virtual storytelling projects can captivate audiences, from educational immersion to community-driven adventures and emotionally resonant narratives. As we explore these successful projects, we gain insights into the creative possibilities and transformative impact of virtual and augmented reality in the realm of storytelling.

Chapter (6) Web Serials and Podcasts

A: The Resurgence of Serialized Storytelling

Serialized storytelling, a time-honored narrative tradition, has experienced a notable resurgence in the digital age. This section of the chapter explores the factors contributing to this revival and the unique characteristics that make serialized storytelling a compelling choice for contemporary audiences.

1. Digital Platforms and Accessibility

In the digital era, storytelling has found a new home on a myriad of platforms. Dedicated websites, streaming services, and social media platforms have become the stages for serialized narratives. This accessibility allows creators to reach a global audience, breaking free from the limitations of traditional publishing or broadcasting.

2. Episodic Format and Audience Engagement

The episodic format of serialized storytelling has proven to be a powerful tool for engaging modern audiences. With the ability to release content in bite-sized episodes, creators can sustain interest over extended periods. This approach not only caters to short attention spans but also fosters a sense of community as audiences eagerly await and discuss each new installment.

3. Diverse Genres and Niche Audiences

The resurgence of serialized storytelling has brought about a diversification of genres and the ability to cater to niche audiences. Creators can explore a wide range of themes and styles, from drama and mystery to fantasy and science fiction. This diversity allows audiences to find narratives that align with their specific interests, fostering a sense of connection and loyalty.

Examples of Successful Serialized Storytelling
a. "Stranger Things" (Streaming Series):

- **Genre:** Science Fiction, Horror
- **Platform:** Streaming Service
- **Success:** "Stranger Things" exemplifies the resurgence of serialized storytelling through its gripping narrative, blending 80s nostalgia with supernatural elements. Released episodically on a streaming platform, the series captures audiences with its mix of mystery, suspense, and character-driven storytelling.

b. "The Witcher" (Streaming Series):

- **Genre:** Fantasy, Adventure
- **Platform:** Streaming Service
- **Success:** Based on the book series, "The Witcher" embraces the serialized format to explore the intricate world of Geralt of Rivia. The episodic release allows viewers to delve into the rich lore and character arcs over multiple installments.

c. "Serial" (Podcast):

- **Genre:** Non-Fiction, True Crime
- **Format:** Podcast
- **Success:** The podcast "Serial" played a pivotal role in popularizing serialized storytelling in the podcasting realm. Each season delves into a true crime case, unraveling the narrative week by week, captivating listeners with its investigative journalism and suspenseful storytelling.

As we navigate the resurgence of serialized storytelling, this chapter invites readers to appreciate the evolving landscape of narrative delivery.

Join us in exploring the diverse stories that unfold episodically, capturing the imaginations of audiences in the digital age.

B: Podcasts as a Storytelling Medium

Podcasts have emerged as a versatile and engaging medium for storytelling, providing audiences with a unique auditory experience. This section of the chapter explores the distinctive characteristics that make podcasts an effective storytelling medium and delves into the reasons behind their growing popularity.

1. Audio Immersion and Imagination

a. Theater of the Mind:

Podcasts leverage the power of audio to create a theater of the mind, allowing listeners to imagine and visualize the narrative without the constraints of visuals. Sound effects, music, and voice acting collaborate to paint vivid mental pictures, fostering a deeply immersive storytelling experience.

b. Personalized Mental Landscapes:

The absence of visual elements in podcasts invites listeners to actively engage their imaginations. Each listener creates a personalized mental landscape, interpreting the story in their unique way. This participatory aspect enhances the connection between the narrative and the audience.

2. Accessibility and Convenience

a. Listening On-the-Go:

One of the key advantages of podcasts is their accessibility. Listeners can enjoy podcasts during various activities, such as commuting, exercising, or doing household chores. The flexibility of podcast consumption aligns with the on-the-go nature of modern lifestyles, making storytelling a part of daily routines.

b. A Broad Range of Topics:

Podcasts cover a broad range of topics and genres, from fiction and non-fiction to news, education, and entertainment. This diversity allows creators to tailor content to niche interests, providing listeners with an extensive array of storytelling options.

3. Diverse Story Formats

a. Scripted Dramas:

Some podcasts feature scripted dramas with intricate plots, character development, and immersive sound design. These scripted narratives bring the storytelling techniques of traditional radio dramas into the digital age, offering a fresh and modern twist.

b. Non-fiction Narratives:

Podcasts excel at delivering compelling non-fiction narratives, such as true crime stories, investigative journalism, and historical accounts. The podcast format allows for in-depth exploration of real-world events, bringing a sense of authenticity to storytelling.

Examples of Successful Podcasts

a. "Serial" (True Crime):

- **Format:** Serialized Podcast
- **Success:** "Serial" captivated audiences with its in-depth exploration of true crime cases. The podcast's investigative journalism approach and episodic release format contributed to its widespread popularity, sparking a renewed interest in podcasts as a storytelling medium.

b. "The Adventure Zone" (Fiction):

- **Format:** Actual Play Podcast (Fiction)
- **Success:** "The Adventure Zone" is a podcast where a family of comedians plays tabletop role-playing games. The unscripted nature of the show, combined with humor and storytelling, showcases the flexibility of podcasts for fiction and entertainment.

c. "TED Talks Daily" (Non-fiction):

- **Format:** Daily Podcast
- **Success:** "TED Talks Daily" brings the world of TED Talks to listeners in a podcast format. The succinct and informative nature of TED Talks aligns well with the podcast medium, allowing for easy consumption of insightful ideas on a daily basis.

As we explore podcasts as a storytelling medium, this chapter invites readers to embrace the auditory journey of narratives and appreciate the dynamic and accessible nature of storytelling through the spoken word. Join us in unraveling the diverse stories that unfold through podcasts, enriching the world of narrative arts.

C: Successful Examples of Web Serials and Podcasts

The landscape of web serials and podcasts is teeming with innovative and captivating storytelling. This section of the chapter explores successful examples of web serials and podcasts that have left a lasting impact on audiences, showcasing the diverse narratives and formats that these mediums offer.

Web Serials:

a. "Stranger Things" (Streaming Series):

- **Genre:** Science Fiction, Horror
- **Platform:** Streaming Service
- **Success:** "Stranger Things" exemplifies the resurgence of serialized storytelling through its gripping narrative, blending 80s nostalgia with supernatural elements. The series captures audiences with its mix of mystery, suspense, and character-driven storytelling.

b. "The Mandalorian" (Streaming Series):

- **Genre:** Science Fiction, Space Western
- **Platform:** Streaming Service
- **Success:** "The Mandalorian" contributed to the resurgence of serialized storytelling in the visual medium. Released episodically on a streaming platform, it captivated audiences with its character-driven narrative set in the "Star Wars" universe.

c. "The Marvelous Mrs. Maisel" (Streaming Series):

Genre: Comedy, Drama

Platform: Streaming Service

Success: This web series follows the journey of a 1950s housewife turned stand-up comedian. The episodic format allows for the exploration of character development and period-specific storytelling, contributing to the show's critical acclaim.

Podcasts:

a. "Serial" (True Crime):

- **Format:** Serialized Podcast
- **Success:** "Serial" captivated audiences with its in-depth exploration of true crime cases. The podcast's investigative journalism approach and episodic release format contributed to its widespread popularity, sparking a renewed interest in podcasts as a storytelling medium.

b. "The Adventure Zone" (Actual Play Podcast - Fiction):

- **Format:** Actual Play Podcast (Fiction)
- **Success:** "The Adventure Zone" is a podcast where a family of comedians plays tabletop role-playing games. The unscripted nature of the show, combined with humor and storytelling, showcases the flexibility of podcasts for fiction and entertainment.

c. "TED Talks Daily" (Non-fiction):

- **Format:** Daily Podcast

- **Success:** "TED Talks Daily" brings the world of TED Talks to listeners in a podcast format. The succinct and informative nature of TED Talks aligns well with the podcast medium, allowing for easy consumption of insightful ideas on a daily basis.

d. "Welcome to Night Vale" (Fiction):

- **Genre:** Fiction, Supernatural

- **Format:** Serialized Podcast
- **Success:** "Welcome to Night Vale" gained a dedicated fan base for its episodic exploration of a fictional town where strange and supernatural events occur. The podcast's success lies in its unique storytelling approach, blending humor, horror, and mystery.

e. "The Black Tapes" (Fiction - Horror):

- Genre: Fiction, Horror
- Format: Serialized Podcast
- **Success:** This podcast follows a journalist investigating unsolved paranormal cases. With a gripping narrative and a mix of horror and suspense, "The Black Tapes" exemplifies how podcasts can create immersive storytelling experiences.

As we explore these successful examples of web serials and podcasts, this chapter invites readers to appreciate the diverse and dynamic nature of these mediums. Join us in unraveling the storytelling renaissance facilitated by accessible digital platforms and the unique narrative possibilities offered by web serials and podcasts.

Chapter (7) Collaborative Storytelling

A: Online Communities and Collaborative Storytelling Platforms

Online communities and collaborative storytelling platforms serve as dynamic spaces where storytellers from around the world converge to weave narratives collectively. This section explores the emergence of digital hubs, interactive storytelling platforms, and the significance of fan fiction communities in the realm of collaborative storytelling.

1. Emergence of Digital Hubs

In the digital age, storytelling has transcended the boundaries of traditional mediums, finding new homes in online communities. These virtual spaces, ranging from social media groups to specialized forums, act as gathering points for individuals passionate about collaborative storytelling. Creators and enthusiasts alike converge to share ideas, co-create narratives, and engage in collective storytelling endeavors.

2. Interactive Storytelling Platforms

Dedicated platforms designed for collaborative storytelling provide structured frameworks that facilitate interaction among contributors. Websites like Wattpad, Story Wars, and Storium offer spaces where users can contribute to ongoing stories, often incorporating elements of role-playing and interactive decision-making. These platforms create a dynamic and evolving narrative landscape shaped by the collaborative efforts of participants.

3. Fan Fiction Communities

Fan fiction communities represent a vibrant and integral aspect of collaborative storytelling. Enthusiastic fans, inspired by existing universes from literature, TV shows, movies, or games, come together to contribute their own creative interpretations and extensions. These communities thrive on shared passion, allowing contributors to explore and expand upon beloved fictional worlds.

- **Online Community Dynamics**

a. Shared Enthusiasm:

Online communities foster shared enthusiasm among participants, creating a sense of belonging and camaraderie. Collaborators connect over a common passion for storytelling and engage in the collective creation of narratives.

b. Open Dialogue and Feedback:

Interactive platforms enable open dialogue and feedback, encouraging contributors to share ideas and respond to each other's contributions. This iterative process enhances the richness of the storytelling experience.

c. Community-Driven Projects:

Collaborative storytelling often evolves into community-driven projects, where individuals collaborate on larger narrative arcs, world-building endeavors, or themed storytelling events. These projects harness the collective creativity of the community.

As we explore the role of online communities and collaborative storytelling platforms, this chapter invites readers to delve into the interconnected and ever-evolving world of digital storytelling. Join us in understanding how these platforms empower individuals to contribute, collaborate, and co-create narratives in the exciting landscape of collaborative storytelling.

B: Crowdsourcing Narratives and Shared World-Building

Crowdsourcing narratives and shared world-building are integral aspects of collaborative storytelling, where the collective creativity of contributors shapes the direction of a story or constructs the foundation of fictional worlds. This section explores the practices of crowdsourcing plot points and engaging in shared world-building projects within the collaborative storytelling landscape.

1. Crowdsourcing Plot Points

a. Democratizing Storytelling:

Collaborative storytelling often involves the democratization of storytelling decisions. Contributors have the opportunity to suggest plot points, twists, or character developments, and the community collectively decides through voting or discussion which direction the narrative should take.

b. Engaging the Audience:

Crowdsourcing plot points engages the audience in a participatory storytelling experience. It empowers contributors to have a direct impact on the unfolding narrative, fostering a sense of ownership and connection to the story.

c. Dynamic and Adaptive Narratives:

The crowdsourcing of plot points introduces an element of dynamism and adaptability to the narrative. As contributors offer diverse ideas, the story can take unexpected turns, creating a living and evolving storyline that reflects the collective imagination of the community.

2. Shared World-Building Projects

a. Constructing Collaborative Universes:

Shared world-building projects involve contributors collectively constructing the elements of a fictional universe. This includes developing the lore, history, geography, and cultural nuances of the world. The collaborative effort ensures a cohesive backdrop for multiple stories to unfold.

b. Diversity in Perspectives:

Shared world-building allows for the integration of diverse perspectives and creative ideas. Contributors bring unique cultural, historical, and imaginative elements to the world, enriching the storytelling experience with a tapestry of influences.

c. Interconnected Story Threads:

In shared world-building, individual contributors may explore different story threads within the same universe. These interconnected narratives create a mosaic of stories, each contributing to the overall richness and depth of the collaborative world.

Practices in Crowdsourcing and Shared World-Building

a. Online Platforms and Tools:

Crowdsourcing and shared world-building often rely on online platforms and tools that facilitate collaborative contributions. This may include dedicated websites, forums, or collaborative writing platforms that allow for real-time interaction.

b. Moderation and Guidelines:

Successful crowdsourcing and shared world-building projects often involve effective moderation and clear guidelines. Moderators help maintain consistency in the narrative, while guidelines provide a framework for contributors, balancing creative freedom with structural coherence.

c. Iterative Creation Process:

The creation process in crowdsourcing and shared world-building is often iterative. Contributors build upon each other's ideas, refining and expanding the narrative through an ongoing and collaborative creative process.

As we delve into the realms of crowdsourcing narratives and shared world-building, this chapter invites readers to explore the dynamic and collective nature of storytelling. Join us in understanding how collaborative efforts shape narratives and build fictional worlds that transcend the boundaries of individual imagination.

C: Challenges and Opportunities in Collaborative Storytelling

Collaborative storytelling presents a unique and dynamic landscape, offering both opportunities for creative exploration and challenges that arise from the diverse voices contributing to a narrative. This section delves into the intricacies of collaborative storytelling, examining the potential pitfalls and the avenues for growth and innovation.

Challenges in Collaborative Storytelling

1. Maintaining Consistency:

One of the primary challenges in collaborative storytelling is maintaining consistency in the narrative. With multiple contributors adding their unique perspectives, ensuring a coherent and cohesive storyline becomes a delicate balancing act.

2. Balancing Creative Freedom and Structure:

Striking a balance between providing contributors with creative freedom and maintaining a coherent structure can be challenging. Establishing clear guidelines and rules becomes essential to prevent diverging storylines that may disrupt the overall narrative.

3. Community Dynamics and Conflict Resolution:

Online communities engaged in collaborative storytelling may experience dynamics and conflicts that can impact the creative process. Effective moderation and conflict resolution mechanisms are crucial to maintaining a positive and inclusive environment for contributors.

Opportunities in Collaborative Storytelling

1. Opportunity for Diverse Perspectives:

One of the significant opportunities in collaborative storytelling lies in the incorporation of diverse perspectives. The collaborative process allows for the integration of varied voices, cultural influences, and storytelling styles, enriching the narrative with a tapestry of experiences.

2. Building a Sense of Community:

Successful collaborative storytelling projects often foster a strong sense of community among contributors. Recognition, engagement, and shared achievements contribute to building a supportive and creative environment where individuals feel connected to a shared purpose.

3. Innovation Through Collective Creativity:

Collaborative storytelling opens the door to innovation through collective creativity. The merging of different ideas and imaginative approaches can lead to unexpected and groundbreaking narratives that may not have emerged through individual storytelling endeavors.

4. Community-Driven Projects:

Collaborative storytelling often evolves into community-driven projects, where contributors collaboratively work on larger narrative arcs, world-building endeavors, or themed storytelling events. These projects leverage the collective talents of the community to create expansive and intricate narratives.

5. Iterative and Adaptive Storytelling:

The iterative nature of collaborative storytelling allows for adaptive and evolving narratives. As contributors build upon each other's ideas, the story takes unexpected turns, creating a dynamic and living narrative that reflects the collective imagination of the community.

Practices for Successful Collaborative Storytelling

a. Effective Moderation:

Successful collaborative storytelling projects implement effective moderation to guide the creative process, enforce guidelines, and resolve conflicts. Moderators play a crucial role in maintaining a positive and inclusive community.

b. Clear Guidelines and Rules:

Establishing clear guidelines and rules is essential to provide a framework for contributors. This helps balance creative freedom with structural coherence, ensuring a consistent and engaging narrative.

c. Regular Community Engagement:

Regular community engagement, through discussions, feedback sessions, and acknowledgment of contributions, fosters a sense of belonging and encourages active participation among contributors.

As we navigate the challenges and opportunities in collaborative storytelling, this chapter invites readers to appreciate the dynamic and interconnected nature of narratives crafted by a collective imagination. Join us in understanding how collaborative efforts shape stories, build worlds, and foster communities in the ever-evolving landscape of collaborative storytelling.

Chapter (8) The Future of Storytelling

A: Emerging Technologies and Their Impact on Storytelling

Emerging technologies are reshaping the landscape of storytelling, ushering in an era of immersive experiences and interactive narratives. This section delves into the impact of cutting-edge technologies on storytelling, exploring how virtual reality (VR), augmented reality (AR), interactive elements, and blockchain are transforming the way stories are conceived and consumed.

1. Virtual Reality (VR) and Augmented Reality (AR)

a. Immersive Storytelling Experiences:

Virtual Reality (VR) and Augmented Reality (AR) are revolutionizing storytelling by providing immersive experiences. VR transports users to entirely virtual worlds, while AR overlays digital elements onto the real world. Both technologies create new dimensions for narrative exploration, allowing audiences to be active participants in the story.

b. 360-Degree Storytelling:

VR enables 360-degree storytelling, where audiences can explore the narrative from any angle. This spatial freedom enhances the storytelling experience, making it more engaging and interactive.

c. Enhanced Realism and Presence:

The realism and presence afforded by VR and AR technologies immerse audiences in the story, creating a sense of being within the narrative. This heightened level of engagement transforms storytelling into a visceral and memorable experience.

2. Interactive Narratives and Gamification

a. Choose Your Own Adventure Evolution:

Interactive storytelling has evolved beyond traditional Choose Your Own Adventure narratives. Advanced interactive elements and gamification techniques allow audiences to make meaningful choices that shape the course of the narrative.

b. Branching Storylines:

Narratives are becoming more dynamic with branching storylines that respond to user choices. This form of storytelling provides a personalized and adaptive experience, offering a different journey for each participant.

c. Role of Gamification:

Gamification elements, such as points, rewards, and challenges, are being integrated into storytelling. This not only enhances engagement but also blurs the lines between traditional narratives and interactive gaming experiences.

3. Blockchain and Decentralized Storytelling

a. Transparent Content Creation:

Blockchain technology introduces transparency and decentralization to content creation. Smart contracts enable fair compensation for contributors, ensuring that creators are recognized and rewarded for their contributions in collaborative storytelling projects.

b. Decentralized Distribution:

Blockchain facilitates decentralized distribution of content, reducing dependence on traditional publishing models. This empowers creators to directly connect with audiences and explore new economic models for storytelling.

c. Immutable Record of Contributions:

The immutability of blockchain ensures a transparent and permanent record of contributions. This fosters trust within collaborative storytelling communities and provides a clear attribution of creative input.

Navigating the Technological Frontier

As we explore the impact of emerging technologies on storytelling, this chapter invites readers to envision a future where narratives transcend conventional boundaries. Join us in navigating the technological frontier, where immersive experiences, interactive narratives, and decentralized storytelling pave the way for innovative and transformative storytelling adventures.

C: The Role of AI in Shaping Stories

Artificial Intelligence (AI) stands at the forefront of revolutionizing storytelling, offering capabilities that extend beyond automation to active participation in the creative process. This section explores the evolving role of AI in shaping stories, from generating content to enhancing creativity and creating interactive characters.

1. AI-Generated Content

a. Automated Content Creation:

AI algorithms are increasingly being utilized to automate content creation, ranging from generating articles and poetry to creating entire narratives. This transformative capability streamlines the storytelling process and offers new avenues for creative exploration.

b. Plot Generation and Idea Exploration:

AI plays a pivotal role in generating plot ideas and exploring narrative possibilities. By analyzing vast datasets and identifying patterns, AI systems can suggest novel plot twists, character arcs, and settings, acting as a collaborative partner for human storytellers.

2. Enhancing Creativity and Collaboration

a. Automating Routine Tasks:

AI assists creators by automating routine and time-consuming tasks, allowing human storytellers to focus on more complex aspects of narrative development. This includes tasks such as data analysis, research, and even basic writing functions.

b. Suggesting Creative Ideas:

AI tools are capable of suggesting creative ideas and elements that can be incorporated into a story. This collaborative approach enhances the creative process by introducing novel concepts and perspectives.

c. Facilitating Collaborative Storytelling:

In collaborative storytelling projects, AI can play a facilitating role by aiding in the coordination of contributions, ensuring consistency, and providing valuable insights to maintain narrative coherence.

3. Interactive AI Characters

a. Dynamic Response to User Interactions:

The integration of AI-driven characters into narratives allows for more interactive storytelling experiences. These characters can dynamically respond to user interactions, adapting their behavior and dialogue in real-time, creating a more responsive and engaging narrative environment.

b. AI-Powered Conversational Agents:

AI-powered conversational agents contribute to interactive storytelling by enabling natural language interactions. These agents can simulate dialogue, answer user queries, and dynamically alter their responses based on the user's choices, creating a more immersive narrative experience.

Navigating the AI-Enhanced Narrative Frontier

As we delve into the role of AI in shaping stories, this chapter invites readers to envision a future where AI and human creativity collaborate to push the boundaries of storytelling. Join us in navigating the AI-enhanced narrative frontier, where innovation, automation, and interactive elements converge to redefine how stories are conceived, developed, and experienced in the digital age.

❖ Conclusion

A: Recap of the Journey from Page to Network

Our exploration has taken us on a transformative journey, traversing the landscape of storytelling from the traditional page to the expansive network. Let us revisit the key waypoints on this enlightening path.

1. Definition of "From Page to Network":

We commenced our journey by defining "From Page to Network," recognizing the shift from traditional forms of storytelling on pages to the dynamic and interconnected narratives within the vast digital network.

2. Historical Overview of Storytelling through Written Pages:

Delving into the annals of history, we explored the roots of storytelling through written pages. From ancient manuscripts to the invention of the printing press, we acknowledged the profound impact of written words on human culture and communication.

3. Power of Printed Words and the Magic of Books:

The journey celebrated the enduring power of printed words and the enchantment found within the pages of books. We recognized how books have been vehicles of imagination, knowledge, and storytelling magic throughout the ages.

4. Classic Storytelling Techniques and Their Endurance:

Examining classic storytelling techniques, we acknowledged their endurance across time. The timeless art of crafting narratives on pages has proven to be a foundation upon which storytelling has evolved.

5. Emergence of Digital Platforms and Their Influence:

The narrative evolved with the emergence of digital platforms, influencing how stories are conceived, consumed, and shared. We witnessed the advent of a new era, where technology became an integral part of the storytelling experience.

6. Interactivity in Storytelling: Choose Your Own Adventure Narratives:

Interactive storytelling took center stage, with Choose Your Own Adventure narratives paving the way for audience engagement. Readers became active participants, steering the course of narratives and influencing outcomes.

7. Evolution of E-books and Audiobooks:

We explored the evolution of storytelling mediums with the rise of e-books and audiobooks. Digital formats brought new dimensions to the reading experience, catering to diverse preferences and lifestyles.

8. Micro-stories on Social Platforms:

The narrative expanded to micro-stories on social platforms, where brevity and immediacy became key. Social media became a canvas for succinct and impactful storytelling, shaping narratives in bite-sized increments.

9. Influencer Culture and Its Impact on Storytelling:

Influencer culture emerged as a defining force, shaping narratives in collaboration with personalities who wielded significant influence. Social media influencers became storytellers, connecting with audiences in novel ways.

10. Role of User-Generated Content in Shaping Narratives:

User-generated content took center stage in the digital storytelling landscape. The collective creativity of online communities became a driving force, contributing to the evolution of narratives in unprecedented ways.

This recap serves as a reminder of the diverse waypoints we encountered on our journey, each contributing to the narrative tapestry that weaves the story of storytelling—from the traditional page to the interconnected network

B: The Ongoing Evolution of Storytelling in the Digital Age

Our exploration of storytelling in the digital age has illuminated a dynamic landscape characterized by continuous evolution and innovation. As we recap this ongoing journey, we recognize the transformative shifts that shape the narrative realm in the digital age.

1. Immersive Storytelling Experiences:

The digital age ushered in immersive storytelling experiences through technologies like virtual reality (VR) and augmented reality (AR). These technologies transported audiences to virtual worlds, breaking the barriers between fiction and reality.

2. Interactive Narratives and Gamification:

Interactivity became a hallmark of digital storytelling, evolving beyond traditional narratives. Gamification elements and advanced interactive storytelling techniques empowered audiences to actively participate in shaping the storyline.

3. Blockchain and Decentralized Storytelling:

Blockchain technology introduced transparency and decentralization to the storytelling ecosystem. It facilitated fair compensation for contributors, decentralized distribution models, and created immutable records of creative contributions.

4. Multimedia Convergence:

The ongoing evolution witnessed a seamless integration of multimedia elements in storytelling. Narratives fluidly moved across written, visual, auditory, and interactive formats, creating a holistic and engaging storytelling experience.

5. Personalized and Adaptive Storytelling:

Advances in data analytics and artificial intelligence paved the way for personalized and adaptive storytelling experiences. Narratives dynamically adjusted based on individual preferences, creating intimate and tailored connections with audiences.

6. Cross-Platform Storytelling:

The digital age fostered cross-platform storytelling, transcending the limitations of individual mediums. Stories unfolded seamlessly across books, movies, podcasts, games, and other formats, creating interconnected and cohesive narrative experiences.

7. AI-Generated Content and Collaboration:

Artificial intelligence (AI) played a crucial role in content creation and collaboration. AI algorithms automated routine tasks, suggested creative ideas, and facilitated collaborative storytelling efforts, marking a harmonious integration of human and machine creativity.

8. Interactive AI Characters:

The integration of AI-driven characters into narratives became a reality, offering more immersive and interactive storytelling experiences. These characters dynamically responded to user interactions, enhancing the responsiveness and engagement of the narrative.

As we reflect on the ongoing evolution of storytelling in the digital age, we embrace the constant state of transformation. The digital realm continues to be a playground for creativity, innovation, and the convergence of diverse storytelling elements. The journey from page to network unfolds as a narrative continuum, with each chapter contributing to the ever-expanding story of storytelling in the digital age.

C: Encouraging Creativity and Exploration in the World of Narrative Arts

As we conclude our exploration of storytelling in the digital age, it is essential to emphasize the significance of fostering creativity and encouraging exploration within the expansive realm of narrative arts. This chapter serves as a call to action, inspiring individuals to actively contribute to the rich tapestry of stories that continue to unfold.

1. Embracing Diverse Voices and Perspectives:

In the world of narrative arts, diversity is a cornerstone of creativity. Encouraging a multitude of voices and perspectives enriches storytelling, bringing forth a mosaic of experiences, cultures, and ideas. Embrace the richness that diversity adds to the narrative landscape.

2. Empowering Storytellers to Innovate:

Innovation thrives in an environment that empowers storytellers to push boundaries. Encourage and support creators to experiment with new formats, technologies, and collaborative approaches. Innovation is the catalyst for the evolution of storytelling.

3. Celebrating Collaborative Endeavors:

Collaborative storytelling is a testament to the collective imagination of communities. Celebrate and foster collaborative endeavors that bring together individuals with diverse skills and backgrounds. These collaborations have the potential to create narratives that resonate across a broad spectrum.

4. Nurturing Emerging Technologies:

Embrace the potential of emerging technologies as tools for storytelling. Whether it's virtual reality, artificial intelligence, or blockchain, these technologies offer new avenues for narrative exploration. Nurturing their integration allows for the creation of groundbreaking and immersive experiences.

5. Supporting Creative Communities:

Creative communities are the heartbeat of narrative arts. Support and nurture these communities, both online and offline, where storytellers can connect, share ideas, and collaborate. Building supportive networks fosters an environment conducive to creativity and exploration.

6. Encouraging Experimentation and Risk-Taking:

Creativity flourishes when storytellers feel free to experiment and take risks. Encourage a culture that values exploration and embraces the unknown. Some of the most groundbreaking stories emerge when creators are unafraid to challenge conventions.

7. Promoting Inclusivity and Accessibility:

Storytelling is most impactful when it is inclusive and accessible to diverse audiences. Encourage initiatives that promote inclusivity, ensuring that narratives are representative of various communities. Accessibility allows stories to reach a broader spectrum of people.

8. Educational Initiatives for Storytelling Skills:

Invest in educational initiatives that equip aspiring storytellers with the skills needed to navigate the digital age. Whether it's traditional storytelling techniques or the latest technological advancements, education lays the foundation for a generation of skilled storytellers.

❖ Embracing the Future of Storytelling

As we encourage creativity and exploration in the world of narrative arts, we invite individuals to be active participants in shaping the future of storytelling. The digital age provides an expansive canvas where every storyteller, regardless of background or experience, has the potential to contribute to the ongoing narrative evolution. Let this call resonate, inspiring a new wave of stories that captivate, challenge, and inspire in ways yet to be imagined.

9 798224 051779